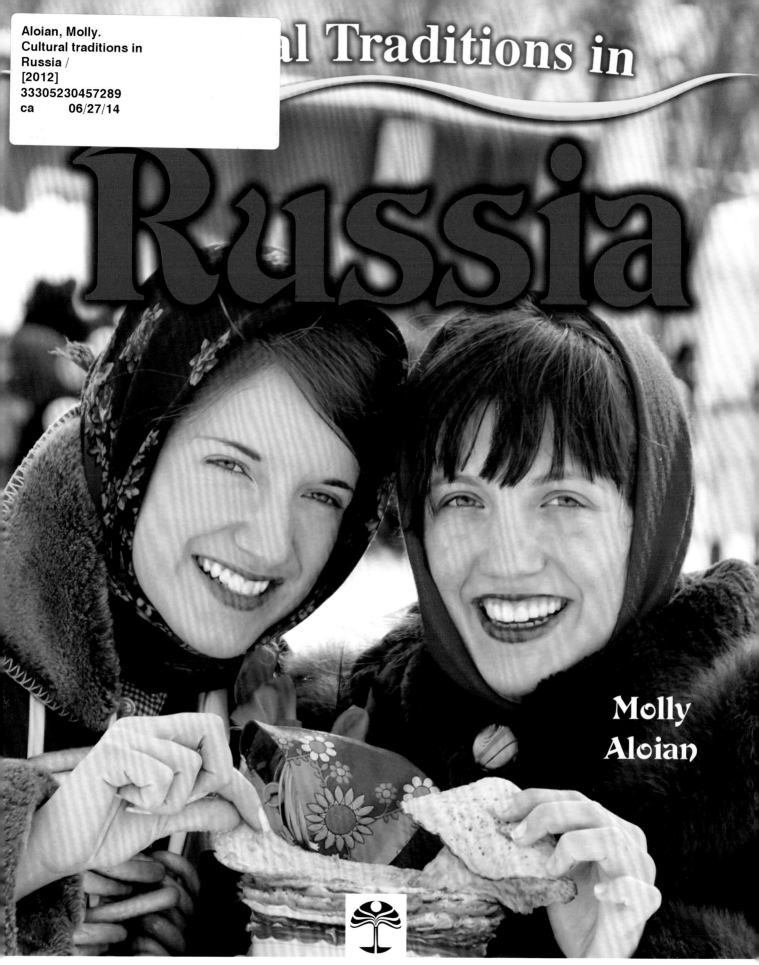

Cultural Traditions in Russia

Russia

Molly
Aloian

Crabtree Publishing Company

www.crabtreebooks.com

Crabtree Publishing Company

www.crabtreebooks.com

Author: Molly Aloian
Publishing plan research and development:
  Sean Charlebois, Reagan Miller
  Crabtree Publishing Company
Project coordinator: Kathy Middleton
Editor: Crystal Sikkens
Proofreader: Kathy Middleton
Photo research: Allison Napier, Crystal Sikkens
Design: Margaret Amy Salter
Production coordinator: Margaret Amy Salter
Prepress technician: Margaret Amy Salter
Print coordinator: Katherine Berti

Cover: St. Basil's Cathedral in Moscow (top); Russian Easter cake (bottom center); scarecrow decoration for the celebration of Shrovetide (middle left); Russian girl in traditional clothing with Easter eggs (middle right); hand-painted Easter eggs (bottom left); a matryoshka, or Russian nesting doll set (bottom right)

Title page: Russian women eating pancakes during Shrovetide

Photographs:
Alamy: ITAR-TASS Photo Agency: pages 11, 26, 29
Sergel Grits / Associated Press: page 25
Dreamstime: Evdoha: cover (middle right); Dimaberkut: page 16; Metlion: pages 30, 31 (right); Bgodunoff: page 31 (left)
iStockphoto: Sharon McIntyre: cover (bottom left)
Shutterstock: cover (bottom right), pages 1, 4, 7 (left), 8, 9, 10–11, 13 (bottom), 15 (top), 18, 24, 28; Dikiiy: cover (middle left); ID1974: pages 5, 23 (top); Tarasenko Sergey: page 7 (right); Limpopo: page 12; joyfull: page 13 (top); Dmitry Berkut: page 14; rook76: page 15 (bottom); withGod: page 22; joppo: page 23 (bottom)
Thinkstock: cover (top, bottom center), pages 6, 17, 27
Wikimedia Commons: Errabee: page 19; Zenonas: page 20 (top); Андрей Романенко: page 20 (bottom); Kostya Wiki: page 21

Library and Archives Canada Cataloguing in Publication

Aloian, Molly
    Cultural traditions in Russia / Molly Aloian.

(Cultural traditions in my world)
Includes index.
Issued also in electronic format.
ISBN 978-0-7787-7588-1 (bound).--ISBN 978-0-7787-7595-9 (pbk.)

    1. Festivals--Russia (Federation)--Juvenile literature.
2. Holidays--Russia (Federation)--Juvenile literature. 3. Russia (Federation)--Social life and customs--Juvenile literature. I. Title.
II. Series: Cultural traditions in my world

GT4856.2.A2A56 2012   j394.26947   C2012-900674-2

Library of Congress Cataloging-in-Publication Data

CIP available at Library of Congress

Crabtree Publishing Company
www.crabtreebooks.com   1-800-387-7650

Printed in Canada / 102013 / MA20130906

Published in Canada
Crabtree Publishing
616 Welland Ave.
St. Catharines, ON
L2M 5V6

Published in the United States
Crabtree Publishing
PMB 59051
350 Fifth Avenue, 59th Floor
New York, New York 10118

Published in the United Kingdom
Crabtree Publishing
Maritime House
Basin Road North, Hove
BN41 1WR

Published in Australia
Crabtree Publishing
3 Charles Street
Coburg North
VIC 3058

Contents

Welcome to Russia

Russia is the largest country in the world. It is over one and half times the size of the United States. Russia stretches over parts of two continents, Europe and Asia. It has a wide variety of environments, climates, and landforms that range from its flat plains to its rolling mountains. There are over 139 million people that live in Russia. Most people live in the European portion around the country's capital city, Moscow.

Did You Know?
Moscow is Russia's largest city. Over 10 million people live in Moscow.

Cultural traditions are the holidays, festivals, and customs that groups of people celebrate each year. Russians celebrate many traditions such as birthdays, graduations, weddings, Christmas, and many other events during the year. People in Russia also celebrate special days and events that are specific to their culture.

Some cultural traditions celebrate an important day in history. Others are religious celebrations, such as this Easter celebration in Moscow.

Happy New Year!

New Year is a very special holiday in Russia because it is a time to celebrate new beginnings. Like people in many other countries, people in Russia celebrate New Year's Eve on December 31 and New Year's Day on January 1. Most people spend the holiday with friends and family.

Many places set off fireworks at midnight on December 31.

Many people in Russia decorate a New Year's tree called *Novogodnaya Yolka*. It is similar to a Christmas tree. It is decorated with various sweets and topped with a bright star. Children anxiously wait for *Ded Moroz*, or Father Frost, and his granddaughter, called *Snegurochka*, to put New Year's presents under the tree.

Did You Know?
A traditional dish served at New Year is olivier salad, or Russian salad. It is made with potatoes, eggs, ham, and vegetables, and mixed in a mayonnaise dressing.

Christmas in Russia

Skating is a favorite pastime in Russia. Many skating rinks open during the Christmas season.

Did You Know?
Most people in Russia follow the Russian Orthodox Church. The Church follows the Julian calendar. According to this calendar, Christmas is on January 7.

In most places in Russia, Christmas is celebrated on January 7. Christmas is part of Russia's Festival of Winter. The Festival of Winter is 39 days long. It starts at the end of November and continues to the evening of January 6. During the Festival of Winter, people exchange gifts, go to parties, go skating, and go tobogganing.

To celebrate Christmas, people go to church and say prayers, and sing hymns and carols. At home, families and friends gather together to eat a 12-course dinner, which includes foods such as fish, cabbage, dried fruit, and beet soup called *borsch*. One of the most traditional Russian Christmas dishes is a special porridge called *kutya*.

Did You Know?
Many Russian families eat *kutya* from a common dish. This is believed to symbolize the **unity** of their family.

Defender of the Motherland Day

On February 23, people in Russia celebrate and honor soldiers who have died, military **veterans**, and active army officers. This day was formerly known as Soviet Army Day. Following the fall of the **Soviet Union** in 1991, it was given its current name and became a day to celebrate anyone who has served in defense of the country.

People often lay flowers on the graves of military soldiers that have died. There are also military parades around the major war **memorials** in Russian cities, as well as other events honoring veterans. In the evening, magnificent displays of fireworks light up the skies in the major city centers.

Maslenitsa

Maslenitsa is a Russian holiday that is celebrated during the last week before Lent or the seventh week before Easter. This holiday also signals the end of winter and marks the beginning of spring. It is a time to feast, especially on buttery, golden pancakes, and enjoy delicious food before meat, dairy, fish, and eggs are forbidden for Lent.

A custom during Maslenitsa is to make a scarecrow, which is used to represent winter, and on the last day of the holiday burn the scarecrow and say good-bye to winter.

Blini are Russian pancakes. People share blini with friends and family during the week of Maslenitsa. They are topped with all kinds of foods including caviar, mushrooms, jam, sour cream, and butter.

Hard biscuits called cracknel are also served on Maslenitsa.

13

Women's Day

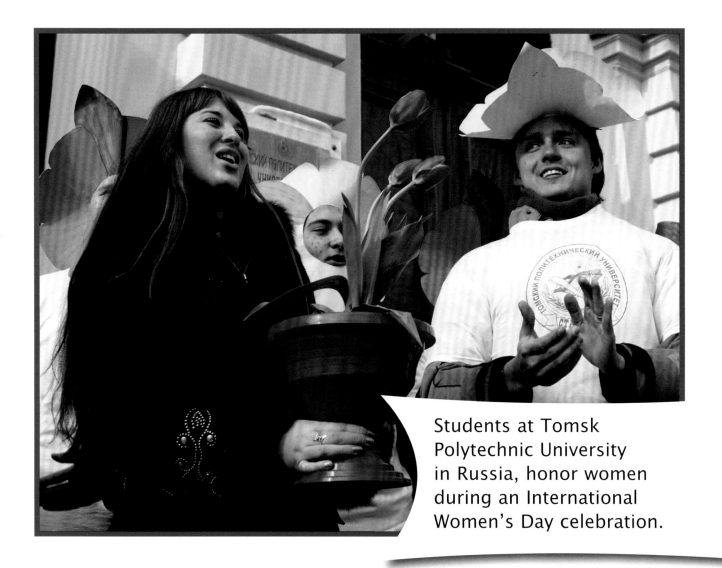

Students at Tomsk Polytechnic University in Russia, honor women during an International Women's Day celebration.

People in Russia celebrate International Women's Day on March 8 each year. Most banks, office buildings, and schools are closed. On this day, people take the time to celebrate and appreciate their mothers, sisters, aunts, and other women in their lives. They honor women's achievements and accomplishments and celebrate **equality**. Russia first observed International Women's Day in 1913.

On Women's Day, many men give flowers, cards, and other small gifts to the women in their lives. The mimosa is a flower that is a symbol for International Women's Day celebrations in Russia. Mimosas grow in large shrubs, which can reach up to 10 feet (3 meters) tall.

Did You Know?
The Soviet cosmonaut Valentina Vladimirovna Tereshkova was the first woman in space. She was on the Vostok 5 mission, which launched on June 16, 1963, and orbited Earth 48 times.

Easter

In Russia, Easter occurs in April or May. Like many others around the world, people in Russia celebrate Easter with special foods and decorated Easter eggs. Families often attend evening church services and then celebrate with an Easter breakfast feast. Some church services are hours long and can last until dawn.

Did You Know?
Christians believe Jesus Christ died on a cross on Good Friday and rose from the dead to live in heaven on Easter Sunday.

These members are proceeding to their church in Moscow for an Easter service.

Paskha is made from cheese and other ingredients, and is usually formed into the shape of a pyramid.

Russians feast on traditional foods at Easter including a sweet type of bread called *kulich* and a spreadable cheese dish called *paskha*. Eggs are another popular Easter food because they are forbidden during Lent. Many people also decorate eggs with beautiful landscapes, churches, scenes from stories, and other designs.

Did You Know?
Easter eggs that are painted red symbolize the blood of Christ.

Cosmonautics Day

People in Russia celebrate Cosmonautics Day on April 12. This holiday celebrates Russia's achievements in the space industry and the first manned space flight made on April 12, 1961, by Yuri Gagarin. Gagarin orbited Earth for one hour and 48 minutes aboard the *Vostok 1* spacecraft. Today, Gagarin is considered a national hero in Russia and is famous around the world.

A **monument** of Yuri Gagarin stands in Komsomolsk-on-Amur, Russia, to remember his achievements.

People visit a memorial for Yuri Gagarin in Cosmonauts Alley on Cosmonautics Day.

Cosmonautics Day celebrations include a special ceremony in Korolyov, which is often referred to as the "cradle of space exploration." People then visit the Kremlin Wall Necropolis in the Red Square, in Moscow, to pay their respects at Yuri Gagarin's grave. Many then proceed through Cosmonauts Alley, which contains **busts** of Yuri Gagarin and other important people in space exploration, such as Sergei Korolyov and Valentina Tereshkova.

Radio Day

In Russia, May 7 is Radio Day. On this day, people celebrate the development and invention of the radio in 1895. On May 7, 1895, a Russian **physicist** named Alexander Stepanovich Popov demonstrated his invention of the radio to the Russian Chemical and Physical Society in St. Petersburg, Russia.

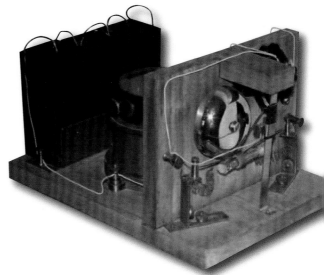

The building (below) where Alexander Stepanovich Popov first tested his radio receiver (above) is still standing in Kronstadt, Russia.

More than 100 years later, the radio is still one of the most popular forms of wireless communication in the world, along with television, mobile communication, and the Internet. In 2009, a **commemorative** plaque made in Popov's honor was unveiled at the International Telecommunications Union (ITU) headquarters in Geneva, Switzerland. The plaque was sited in the ITU's tower building and a conference room was named in honor of Popov.

A monument honoring Alexander Stepanovich Popov stands in Krasnoturyinsk, Russia.

Victory Day

May 9 is Victory Day in Russia. This day is one of the most important holidays in Russia. It commemorates the day in 1945 that Germany surrendered to the Soviet Union during World War II (1939-1945). Germany's surrender ended one of the bloodiest wars in Russia's history and millions of Russians died defending their country.

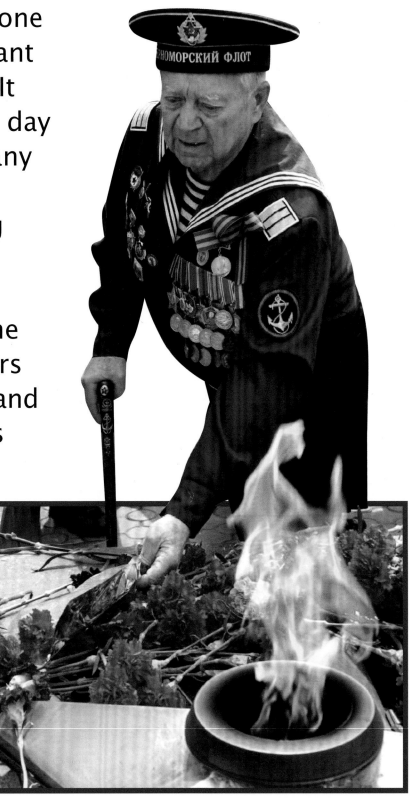

A war veteran pays tribute to fallen soliders on Victory Day.

On this day, TV networks broadcast World War II-inspired films, younger generations honor veterans with red carnations, and many people lay wreaths at war memorials. At night, huge crowds of people gather to watch the fireworks at the Red Square.

Thousands of people attend a military parade at the Red Square in Moscow on Victory Day. Most veterans wear their medals at the parade.

Russia Day

People celebrate Russia Day on June 12. This day marks the day Russia declared its independence from the Soviet Union. On this day, people celebrate Russia's **economic** and **social** achievements. They may also pay tribute to famous Russians, including scientists, writers, and artists. Most banks, offices, and schools are closed on Russia Day.

Did You Know?
Russia Day is one of the newest holidays. It became a public holiday in 1992.

Fireworks light up the sky in the evening of Russia Day.

On Russia Day in 2006, 40,000 environmentalists marched along the main street in Moscow. They were marching to encourage the public to become more aware of the many environmental issues in Russia. They mixed their pleas to the public with **declarations** of national pride.

Did You Know?
On Russia Day, banners reading "Russia Forward!" and "Glory to Russia" are strung above the streets.

People march through downtown Moscow on Russia Day in 2006.

Ivan Kupala Day

June 24 of the Julian calendar marks the day of summer solstice known as Ivan Kupala Day. Long ago, June 24 was the first day of the year when the Orthodox Church allowed bathing and swimming in rivers and ponds. Today, many young people perform pranks, such as throwing water at unsuspecting people, or participate in water fights.

A ritual of Ivan Kupala Day is for girls to float flower wreaths down a river. The pattern that their flowing wreaths make gives them their fortune for future relationships.

According to legend, one should not sleep during the night of Ivan Kupala, as it is the time when evil spirits, such as witches, werewolves, water nymphs, and wood goblins, become active. People light huge bonfires on this night to ward off these evil spirits.

Did You Know?
Unmarried girls wear flower garlands in their hair on Ivan Kupala Day.

National Unity Day

The people of Russia celebrate their sense of national unity on November 4 each year. On Unity Day, people honor and celebrate the many ethnic and religious groups in Russia and their sense of togetherness as a country.

Did You Know?
A merchant named Kuzma Minin and a prince named Dmitry Pozharsky are national heroes in Russia. They defended their country against a Polish invasion on November 4, 1612. In 1649, this day became a public holiday.

РАЖДАНИНУ МИНИНУ И КНЯЗЮ ПОЖАРСКОМУ
БЛАГОДАРНАЯ РОССІЯ. ЛѢТА 1818

People gather on Unity Day to display a blanket of peace created to symbolize harmony among Russia's ethnic groups.

Russians celebrate Unity Day in many ways. Some people bring flowers to the monuments of their national heroes. Politicial, religious, and public figures give speeches stressing the importance of **tolerance** between ethnic and religious groups. Others attend concerts or other public events.

Other Holidays

Many ethnic groups in Russia have their own holidays and festivals. In summer, the Buryats celebrate Surkharban after important crops have been sown. **Muslims** living in Asian Russia celebrate a festival called Navruz. Navruz celebrates the arrival of spring. The Tatars is a large ethnic group found in Russia. They celebrate a summer festival called Sabantuy.

Tatars dress in ethnic clothing and perform cultural dances on Sabantuy. Many also sell traditional clothes and crafts.

The main components of Sabantuy include traditional sporting competitions such as wrestling, horse racing, sack races, pillar-climbing, egg-in-spoon-in-mouth-racing, the three-legged race, and other games and activities. These activities usually take place at a location near the edge of a forest.

Did You Know?
Tatars originally came from Turkey. Today, they live throughout Russia, and in other countries such as Australia, Canada, Germany, and the United States.

Glossary

busts Sculptures of the upper parts of people including the head and neck

commemorative To act as a reminder of something; to remember or honor

declaration To proclaim, or publicly announce

economic Relating to the production, distribution, and consumption of goods and services

equality The state of being equal or exactly the same

memorial Something that keeps alive the memory of a person or event

monument Something that serves as a memorial or a place of historic interest

Muslims People who follow the Islam religion

physicist A scientist that studies matter and energy

social Relating to human society

Soviet Union A former communist country that included Russia and 14 other republics; also known as the USSR

tolerance Accepting feelings, habits, or beliefs that are different from one's own

unity The quality or state of being one

veteran A person who has served in the armed forces

Index